The Role of the Kindergarten Teacher in the Classroom

Mary Bertha Brown

authorHOUSE®

AuthorHouse™
1663 Liberty Drive
Bloomington, IN 47403
www.authorhouse.com
Phone: 1-800-839-8640

First published by AuthorHouse 4/6/2010

ISBN: 978-1-4490-5668-1 (e)
ISBN: 978-1-4490-5667-4 (sc)

Library of Congress Control Number: 2010901349

Printed in the United States of America
Bloomington, Indiana

This book is printed on acid-free paper.

To Kindergarten Teachers
and
Parents of Young Children
with Thanks

Table of Contents

Introduction

This book is written mainly for teachers of kindergarten children. We as educators know that early childhood is the most critical period in human growth and development of young children. We also know that the concentration of our educational resources during these early years yield probably the greatest return of any investment we can make as teachers of kindergarten children.

The early years of young children are so crucial - the period when the foundation for learning is laid - the quality of early learning experiences for young children must be excellent. The kindergarten teacher must be diverse, creative, well planned and managed to give each child the developmental experiences necessary before beginning the formal learning process. A solid beginning in kindergarten will enhance each individual's potential for later school success.

As kindergarten teachers we know learning is an essential part of every child's life. Play and exploration are natural parts of children's need to learn and to satisfy their curiosity about the world around them. Therefore, if we desire to enable each child to learn more, time for the kindergarten teacher must provide learning and appropriate play material for it.

The roles of the kindergarten teachers are very challenging and rewarding.

Foreword

Early childhood educators from the classroom have helped me develop this book. As an educator works of Piaget, James Hymes, and Marie Montessori inspired me.

Beginning teachers as learners take center stage in a curriculum framework. Their cognitive, affective and psychomotor development has received careful attention with transdiscipline plan for instruction. Each kindergarten teacher will be acutely aware that a student's future attitude toward learning is often determined by early educational experiences.

Secondly to kindergarten teachers this book will supply suggestions and recommendations for assessing and managing the environment, the entry level and progress of each youngster and the quality of the prescribed learning experiences.

Thirdly this book has been prepared with the hope that it will provide some practical suggestions for those teachers of young children who are searching for more effective learning strategies.

Teaching Kindergarten in the Classroom

Teachers who have taught kindergarten often say that it is helpful to anticipate frustrations during the transition period.

The traditionally trained teacher if often disconcerted by children moving around, an increased noise level, not knowing exactly what each child is doing at every minute, and the uncertainty of her own role. These and other reasons suggest a gradual transition for most of us!

Not all teachers or children will need this period of gradual transition. Recent graduates and other teachers trained or experienced with this organization for instruction can implement the kindergarten classroom much more rapidly.

These five-year-olds find the structured and unstructured setting "play at your centers and keep your voices down" classroom strange, but very comfortable. Ideally, their kindergarten classroom will be set up in centers from the beginning of the year until the end.

The children to begin with will have a gradual approach playing in small groups at all of the centers except the art and writing centers. Every child will experience success here and much adult supervision will be needed if materials are accessible for the children. (Planning!)

At this point, it seems wise to offer children a choice of several centers. A check-off list of names for the use of the centers can be filled in by a teacher's aid.

Through observation of the children's participation the teacher will determine when the next expansion will occur (probably after several weeks with the other two centers). At this time, a daily period should be scheduled (30-35 minutes or possibly an hour), when the children may freely interact with materials and other people in the room which interest them.

The teacher will have many materials available to stimulate interest. Her primary role, however, is again that of an observer. She should quietly watch the children and offer help only when it is requested. This task will not be an easy one (Patience!) But it's essential for the teacher to gain insights into the interests, skills, work habits, and learning styles of individual children. As she observes the children, the teacher will find it helpful to make notes about the activities of each individual on index cards.

These transitional periods also serve to help children adjust gradually to handling a large degree of freedom and to build positive attitudes towards the learning experience approach. It's fun to learn this way!

When the teacher observes that the children are actively involved in learning this way and she is more comfortable with her role, it is time to expand further.

A successful learning environment meets the children's needs and interests. In order to accomplish this goal, the teacher must assume an active role with the children. The teacher actively plans, implements and evaluates the learning environment each day.

Organizing the Learning Environment for the Children

The next stage that the kindergarten teachers must provide is adequate materials, equipment and support of the parents and principal in a particular school or center.

The teachers use planning to organize larger units of activity for the children (e.g., developing videos, paints, books and objectives) and to provide an overall framework for the children's growth activities.

Organizing the Learning Environment for the Children

By scheduling daily planning times, both the teacher and the teacher's assistant can participate in organizing the next school day. During the planning sessions, the teaching staff should:

- review and record the children's responses and growth within the classroom environment on a daily basis;
- review the organization of materials and centers;
- review the children's use of equipment and materials;
- identify specific objectives, from a continuum of objectives, which will reinforce and/or extend the children's growth and learning;
- develop classroom organization and activity to promote the children's growth;
- select methods for recording children's performance within active learning settings.

Consistent planning provides for the following:

- physical, intellectual and affective areas of the children's development;
- individualized needs of the children;
- children's past experiences in and our of school;
- children's involvement in the planning and assessment process;
- supportive interaction between adults and children.

In meeting the individualized needs, the kindergarten teacher will:

- interact with individual children;
- observe individual children;
- give suggestions to a child needing help;
- assist children in evaluating their own work;
- record a child's progress

In using children's past and present experiences, the kindergarten teacher will:

- provide activities in which children practice skills or concepts previously learned;
- children's involvement in the planning and assessment process;
- supportive interaction between adults and children.

In meeting the individualized needs the kindergarten teacher will do the following:

- provide activities in which children practice skills or concepts previously learned;
- use past experience (e.g. language, travel, food) as a background for learning;
- develop the physical environment (e.g. bulletin boards, books, equipment) to reflect the children's cultural background;
- use children's out-of-school interests (e.g. TV programs, toys) as themes for activities.

By involving children in the planning and assessment process, the teacher will be able to:

- provide whole group, small group or individual time for children to talk about what they have done in the classroom;
- encourage children to suggest activity themes and materials to include in the classroom;
- provide opportunities for children to develop guidelines for participation in learning activities;

In supporting interaction between the teacher and the child, the teacher should:

- listen to children's ideas;
- verbally acknowledge and reinforce children's activities;
- accept the language and ideas of the children;
- extend children's ideas by adding information to the experiences that they discuss.

The initial last step for the kindergarten teacher is the evaluation phase of the program involves both the teaching staff and the children. As children increasingly are involved in planning activities, the children should actively assess those activities they have planned.

Individual, small group and large group settings can be used for evaluation purposes. Honest and open feedback to children is important and should always be coached in positive consideration of future planning.

The continuum of program objectives establishes the basis for on-going evaluation. A systematic record of children's growth assures a proper match between program activity and child growth. More specific recommendations for record keeping and evaluation are contained under "Assessing Child Growth in a Kindergarten Program."

The Teaching Process

The first step in the teaching process is getting to know each individual child. Set up individual conferences with the children. Conduct individual conferences with the parents of the children.

The teacher should give each individual child in the classroom a diagnosis test to determine the learning abilities of the children. The teacher should group the children according to learning abilities and capacities. The groups should be very small because five-year-old children have a short attention span.

After the children have been tested and grouped, the teacher will begin to teach basic skills to the children. The teacher will teach these basic skills step by step because with small children it should be time consuming.

In order to teach basic skills to the children, the teacher must have supplies and materials available to stimulate interest in the young children. The classrooms should be very colorful, bright, and the teacher should have many ideas to stimulate the learning capacities of the children.

The teacher should have an independent learning period during one hour of each day, and other centers to concentrate on a curriculum area, such as language arts. The teacher should begin to work with small groups in the learning centers.

The teacher should use the center approach in a particular area such as language arts, adding centers for other curriculum areas (math, science, etc.) gradually over a period of time. The time block for working in centers increases as new centers are added.

The teacher should team up with another teacher to set up centers for one of several areas of curriculum, and share instructional space and major responsibilities.

The kindergarten teacher should teach the children how to get along with each other, use materials dexterously, express himself of herself confidently, listen intelligently, and follow directions. The teacher should teach health, safety habits, and introduce the children to school life.

The teacher should teach the children how to look at pictures and handle books, read stories to them and sometimes write down the stories they make up. The children are taught how to recognize their names. Through labels on materials they begin to identify names of objects, and thus become familiar with symbols. By taking part in conversations and discussions, with the teachers their vocabulary is widened. These language experiences build a background for reading.

Kindergarten children are taught the use of numbers in a practical way when they count other children and objects. they learn concepts such as big, little, more, less, many, few, high, and low. They are taught the numbers in rhymes and songs and use them correctly in many activities, such as playing store.

Good kindergarten teachers will encourage and stimulate the growth and interest of young children by planning many daily activities for them.

Scheduling

A plan schedule should be a program for five-year-old children. Program scheduling for five-year-olds must meet the following:

(1) the developmental needs of the children;
(2) the increase of maturity levels of these children as the year progresses, and;
(3) the physical structure of the classroom.

Developmentally, young children respond best to programs that provide a balance between:

- exploration/discovery and group activities;
- individual activities and group activities;
- creative arts and academic fields;
- being listened to and listening;
- vigorous play and less active play;
- large muscle activities and small muscle activities;
- first hand experiences and vicarious experiences;
- outdoor activities and indoor activities;
- the three domains.

The kindergarten teacher will see that an adequate balance of activities in the program will encourage and support children to participate in self-initiated and self-regulated activities. Within the limits of the environment structured by the teacher, the children learn to make independent choices for his/her activity and to take independent responsibility for completing the activity. The following program schedules are presented for your consideration.

Modifications of any of these schedules are encouraged to assure maximum flexibility in relating to children's needs. Specific times are not indicated on these schedules. As much as possible, large blocks of time should be used to implement program activities since the time allotted for any activity will vary from day to day, a flexible schedule will allow for this variation.

Suggested Daily Schedule(s)

Double Session Kindergarten (3 hours)

Morning Session (8:30 - 11:30)

30 minutes ----- Greeting the children, conversation, planning, moving activity

45 minutes ----- Toilet

----- Snack

----- Outdoor play

75 minutes ----- Learning centers

30 minutes ----- Clean-up

----- Total group discussion of the day

----- Dismissal

60 minutes ----- Teacher/Aide planning

Double Session Kindergarten (3 hours)

Morning Session (8:00 - 11:00)

20 minutes ----- Arrival and greetings

----- Hang up wraps

----- Breakfast snack

40 minutes ----- Total group planning the day (decisions include indoor and outdoor activities)

----- Rhythm activities and songs

90 minutes ----- Learning centers (self-regulated snack may be set up at a center

----- Clean up

30 minutes ----- Whole group planning and evaluation

----- Story reading

----- Fingerplays and songs

----- Dismissal

60 minutes ----- Teacher/Aide planning, preparation

----- Lunch

Afternoon Session (12:00 - 3:00)

[Repeat morning schedule]

60 minutes ----- Teacher/Aide planning

Double Session Kindergarten (2 ½ hours)

Morning Session (8:00 - 11:30)

30 minutes ----- Greeting the children, conversation, planning
movement activity

30 minutes ----- Toilet

----- Snack

----- Outdoor play

60 minutes ----- Leaning centers

30 minutes ----- Clean-up

----- Total group discussion of the day

----- Dismissal

60 minutes ----- Teacher/aide planning

----- Preparation

----- Lunch

Afternoon Session (12:30 - 2:30)

Repeat morning schedule

60 minutes ----- Teacher/aide planning

Suggested Daily Schedule

Double Session Kindergarten (2 ½ hours)

Morning Session (8:00 - 11:30)

30 minutes ----- Greeting the children, conversation, planning movement activity

30 minutes ----- Toilet

----- Snack

----- Outdoor play

60 minutes ----- Learning centers

30 minutes ----- Clean-up

----- Total group discussion of the day

----- Dismissal

60 minutes ----- Teacher/aide planning, preparation

----- Lunch

Afternoon Session (12:30 - 2:30)

Repeat morning schedule

60 minutes ----- Teacher/Aide planning

Suggested Schedule

Full Day Program with Breakfast

Full Day Session

1 hour ----- Children arrive

A choice of activities available for the children - serve Breakfast, family style. Adults sit with children to encourage natural conversation.

----- Toileting

----- Brushing of teeth

1 ½ hours ----- Total group of discussion of day's activities

----- Learning centers - adults work with individuals or small groups

----- Clean-up

----- Total group story-time and discussion of morning activities

1 hour ----- Outdoor activity

----- Wheel toys

----- Woodworking

----- Art activities

----- Sand and water play and other materials suitable for outdoor use

----- Clean-up

----- Prepare for lunch

1 hour ----- Lunch

----- Toileting

----- Brushing of teeth

----- Story-time in small groups or videos

1 hour ----- Rest (children who are not asleep after 20 minutes
are allowed to engage in quiet self-directed activities.

(One adult remains in room - other adult's plan)

1 ½ hours ----- Learning centers (beverage and snack are
available at one of the centers)

----- Clean-up

----- Total group to make plans for tomorrow, discuss
day and sing

1 ½ hours ----- Parents begin picking up children (children work
in the outdoor or indoor classroom until parents
arrive)

----- Adults plan

LEARNING CENTER

BLOCK BUILDING CENTER

Learning Centers

First of all a learning center is a place where a child goes to do his work. The teacher or aide oversees that the child is doing his or her work in the centers.

The center should contain a variety of learning materials. A center may be set up to accommodate one child or a small group of children at a time. A child may work along or cooperatively with one or more of his peers. While working in a center, a child may or may not receive guidance from an adult.

Work in certain centers may be assigned and required by the teacher. Work in other centers should be chosen freely by each child. Some choices should be offered daily.

Learning centers efficiently and effectively organize learning activities for children. Each learning center is usually limited to two to five children. The number of learning centers present in the classroom at any one time depends on the number of children in the classroom, the ability of the children to select from a number of choices and the children's interests and needs.

Learning centers will be developed gradually. As the year progresses, the kindergarten teacher increasing variety and challenge adds more materials. Children will need time to explore and get acquainted with their environment. The schedule should allow at least one hour for learning center activities in order to provide the opportunity for a child to work in several centers or to carry out an extended project in one center.

Within this framework the teacher will have opportunities to work with individual children or groups of children.

ART CENTER

WRITING CENTER

Each learning center is organized around a theme. Suggested themes include:

- an event such as Halloween, birthday, trip to outer space;
- an activity such as art, cooking, games, woodworking;
- skill and concept development such as sorting, matching, discrimination.

Theme selection allows the teacher to develop a number of related activities options. These activity options generally account for a range of sophistication on the part of the children and offer choices from which children may independently select their activity.

Centers may be established to facilitate more learning experiences:

- a curriculum area: such as math, science, computer;
- development of a specific skill: such as listening, word attack, sequence of events;
- in a combination of disciplines: such as art and music, math and science;
- to foster social development: such as cooperative play, sharing materials, taking turns;
- to meet emotional needs: such as to be alone, to deal with anger, to handle aggression, to think, to express creative ideas, to promote accurate and positive concepts;
- to have FUN!
- To enhance physical development: such as eye-hand coordination, small muscle development, large muscle development, agility, balance.

Teachers experienced with centers often say that it is helpful to anticipate frustrations during the transitional period.

The traditionally-trained teacher is often disconcerted by children moving around, an increased noise level, not knowing exactly what each child is doing at every minute, and the uncertainty of her own role. These and other reasons suggest a gradual transition for most of us.

Not all teachers or children will need this period of gradual transition. Recent graduates and other teachers trained or experienced with this organization for instruction can implement learning centers much more rapidly.

These transitional periods also serve to help children adjust gradually to handling a larger degree of freedom and to build positive attitudes towards the learning center approach. It's fun to learn this way!

When the teacher observes that the children are actively involved in learning this way and she is more comfortable with her role, it is time to expand further.

LIBRARY/BOOK CENTER

Developing Units of Activities

By organizing learning centers and classroom activities according to unit themes or areas of content the teacher may more easily coordinate a set of activities aimed at all areas of development (intellectual, physical and affective). The process of developing a unit is described in the following five basic steps:

Step 1. Select a unit theme bases on one or more of the following sources.

- Long range program goals (e.g. development of number understanding)
- Curriculum content suggested by a local school district (e.g. safety)
- Interests of the children (e.g. cartoon figures)
- Cultural background of the children (e.g. special holiday)

Step 2. Formulate general unit objectives

- These content oriented objectives increase understanding about the unit theme by relating general information or skills to that unit theme

Step 3. Formulate intermediate unit objectives

- Although related to the general unit objectives, these are directed more specifically at the children's developmental needs described in the program domains (physical, intellectual, affective)
- Consider the classroom range of ability in the three domains. Based on the information regularly maintained in the assessment scope of intermediate objectives

Step 4. Develop learning centers and activities, which relate to all of the following:

- Unit theme
- Unit content
- Intermediate objectives

Specify a range of activities within each learning center to support development of specific objectives.

Step 5. Assess children's growth as related to unit objectives. The following sample unit more specifically illustrates the five-step process for developing unit activities.

Unit theme: The Pets

> Rationale for unit theme selection. One of the little boy's cats just had kittens. This stimulated much sharing among the children about their pets. It is also one of the units recommended in the Science Curriculum Guide used by school systems.

General unit objectives

- To find similarities and differences among kinds of pets and between pets and people (e.g. physical characteristics, foods they eat, where they live, how they move).
- To increase familiarity with many and unusual kinds of pets (e.g. cats, puppies, rabbits, birds, snakes, lambs, dogs, kittens, and squirrels).
- To increase understanding of what pets need to live (e.g. food, shelter, and water).
- Intermediate objectives
- Physical – The child will increase development of arm/hand precision
- Affective – The child will increase ability to respond to others
- Intellectual – The child will increase ability to
  (1) Communicate with others,
  (2) Numerate,
  (3) Observe and classify,
  (4) Cooperate with others.

Learning Center Activities

The following is a sample grid that may be used for organizing specific objectives and activities:

Learning Centers And Activities	Physical Development	Intellectual Development	Affective Development

1. Learning Center

Activity A

Activity B

Activity C

17

2. Learning Center

Activity A

Activity B

Activity C

The following is a sample unit or 1-4 day's work:

Learning Centers	Physical Development	Intellectual Development	Affective Development
1. Construction Center	Arm/hand Precision	Uses descriptive vocabulary Complete Project	Works with group to
* Build a zoo out of blocks	(manipulating blocks)		

==

2. Library Center	Turning pages	Classifying and Observing. Uses language frequently and with enjoyment	Responds to limits
* Provide a collection of books for children to explore independently			
* Adult will read animal stories to children		Memory Labeling in small groups	Cooperates and responds
* Children may listen to cooking Center	Arm/hand precision	Recall Labeling	
*Make animal cookies	Arm/hand Precision	Uses descriptive vocabulary Observing Project	Works with group to complete

==

3. Math Center

* Count the animals in a variety of pictures	Handles pictures	Recognizes sets of 1, 2, 3	Responds to indoor limits

* Develop class graph Recording kinds of pets children have	Eye/hand and arm/hand coordination	Count squares in a row on graph, compare "most", "fewer", "more", "least"	Participates and shares with others

===

Discovery Center

Learning Centers	Physical Development	Intellectual Development	Affective Development
* Discuss pictures and label a variety of animals	Fill water jars and food bowls	Observing Use of language Use of descriptive vocabulary	Works cooperatively with group
* Explore a variety of wooden animals. Discuss with adults	Small muscles	Label, compare, recall characteristics of animals	Willingness to participate
* View video tapes On "zoo animals" and "pets"		Label, compare, recall characteristics of animals	Motivation to listen
* Share photographs of pets children have. Develop a display using these photographs	Fine motor arm/hand precision	Communication Labeling Comparing and others.	Willingness to participate Valuing self

===

1. Communications Center

* Dictate tape recorder stories about animals	Punches buttons on tape recorder	Observing, classifying Uses descriptive vocabulary	Listen to another child

Assessment

The teacher will record growth of each child's participation in unit activities through the ongoing assessment checklists for all three areas of development. During daily planning sessions, classroom staff should share observations about specific children and share work completed by individual children.

Physical Environment

The physical environment of the classroom can greatly determine the program's effectiveness. Maintaining standards for a safe, healthy kindergarten classroom, therefore, is tremendously important to the program. Suggested standards have been organized into the following broad areas: (1) adult/child ratio and staff, (2) indoor environment, (3) outdoor environment, (4) safety standards and, (5) health standards.

Adult/Child Ratio and Staff

- The adult/child ratio in each classroom should range from 1:10 to 1:15
- There should be a maximum of 25 students per session enrolled
- Each classroom will be staffed by one state certified teacher and one teacher's aide

In selecting appropriate activities to further the physical development of kindergarten children, the following developmental characteristics should be considered:

- Development of motor skills occurs in approximately the same sequence, bbut not at the same rate
- All children do not automatically become skilled in physical activities

There is a need for practice and adult guidance or instruction.

- Children are naturally active; they need opportunities to explore movement possibilities by moving freely
- Development of fundamental movements (running, jumping, throwing, catching, balancing), occurs primarily during the pre-school years

Regardless of the specific activities planned to enhance physical development, the role of the adult is crucial in creating a climate in which children can develop controlled, physically fit bodies.

The effective teacher should provide a learning environment in which:

- children are active most of the time;
- competition is minimized;
- children are provided with a variety of interesting and challenging activities;

20

- appropriate types and amounts of equipment are available;
- individual efforts are recognized and mistakes are treated as a natural part of the learning process;
- all children are encouraged to participate at their own level of skill-creative approaches to movement problems are encouraged;
- all children are encouraged to evaluate their own performances

The kindergarten teacher should encourage and should guide the efforts of children to use movement as a means to control and adjust to their environment. As children become competent in a variety of physical skills, they develop a sense of self-confidence and security that leads them to initiate new physical experiences.

Although many activities will be initiated by the teacher to develop new skills, more activities should be presented so children may practice and generalize these skills in a variety of settings. Many of the learning centers described in Learning Environment can provide this necessary practice. In the Construction Center, children can integrate gross and fine motor skills as they handle a variety of materials. In the Art Center, children will use arms and fingers as they manipulate brushes, scissors, crayons and clay. Children participating in the Game Center will also practice fine motor skills as they manipulate game pieces, dice and spinners. Children will develop arm and hand control as they handle books in the Library Center. Although motor behavior of some sort will be practiced in virtually every classroom activity, the teacher should be sure that each child has opportunities to develop a range of these skills.

Young children do not develop physically just by eating properly. Like all other areas of the curriculum, physical environment depends on experiences that enhance growth. Young children should have a kind of program including large and small muscle movement, as well as moving through space and balancing.

Pulling, piling, lifting, climbing, riding, pounding, and throwing are some of the large muscle skills that the young child can learn through the environment at school.

Planned exercises should be included in the physical environment program. Exercising with the total body builds strength and confidence. Unfortunately, there aren't many exercises in watching television or other quiet activities expected of children in most homes.

In this component on physical environment, activities are given in all areas previously discussed so teachers can aid the development of all the muscles needed by a growing child.

The teacher will need to consider that no two children are at the same level of development at the same time. Some come to school knowing how to skip, hop, and cut with scissors, for example. Others may not know how to perform many of the physical skills. The solution is to accept the children as they are and to give them the experiences needed to learn the skills they lack.

Experience is the great teacher of us all. How many adults say that they can't perform the simplest of dance steps? What they lack is a good teacher and some experience with these steps. Most do not lack coordination or adequate muscular development.

Kindergarten teachers of young children are responsible for the initial training of Olympic stars and great pointers as well as those of us who will never excel in sports or art. A total physical environment program helps both the future athlete and the business executive.

Resources

Bereiter, C. and Englemann, S. Teaching Disadvantaged in the Preschool. Englewood Cliffs, New Jersey: Prentice-Hall, Inc., 1966

Cohen, O. H. and Rudolph, M. Kindergarten and Early Schooling. Englewood Cliffs, New Jersey: Prentice-Hall, Inc., 1977.

Croft, D. J. and Hess, R. D. An Activities Handbook for Teachers of Young Children. Boston: Houghton Mifflin Co., 1975.

Fallen, N. H. with McGovern, J. H. Young Children with Special Needs. Columbus, Ohio: Charles E. Merrill Publishing Co., 1978.

Fleming, B. M. and Hamiltion, D. S. Resources for Creative Teaching in Early Childhood Education. Atlanta: Harcourt brace Jovanovich, 1977.

Lillie, D. L. Early Childhood Education: An Individualized Approach to Developmental Instruction. Chicago: Science Research Association, 1975.

Petreshene, S. S. Complete Guide to Learning Centers. Palo Alto, California: Pendragon
House, Inc., 1978.

Platts, M. E. LAUNCH: A Handbook of Early Learning Teachniques for the Preschool and Kindergarten Teacher. Stevenville, Michigan: Educational Service, Inc., 1972.

Roberts, V. Playing. Learning and Living. London: A & C Black, Ltd., 1971.

Rounds, S. Teaching the Young Child: A Handbook of Open Classroom Practice. New York: Agathon Press, 1975.

Schickendanz, J. A., York, M. E., Stewart, I. S. and White, D. Strategies for Teaching Young Children. Englewood Cliffs, New Jersey: Prentice-Hall, Inc., 1977.

Silberman, C. E. (Ed). The Open Classroom Reader. New York: Random House, 1973.

Spodik, B. Teaching in the Early Years (2nd Ed.) Englewood Cliffs, New Jersey: Prentice-Hall, Inc., 1978.

Todd, V. E. and Heffernan, H. The Years Before School: Guiding Preschool Children. (3rd Ed.) New York: Macmillan Company, 1977.

Watrin, R. and Furfey, P. H. Learning Activities for the Young Preschool Child. New York: D.Van Nostrand Company, 1978.

Providing Needs for Special Children

The State Board of Education of all states hereby have adopted a policy of providing a free appropriate public education opportunity to all handicapped children within the states of the United States. Public law 94-142 was drafted to govern and educate all handicapped children.

Recognition of Need

The kindergarten teachers recognizing those children who are not succeeding in the range of available activities provided in the classroom is a first step to providing for the educational needs of all children in the classroom. This recognition should signal to the classroom teacher a need to carefully observe and assess the child in an attempt to determine the cause(s) of the child's lack of success in this activity. At early ages, lack of success in school type activities may appear as a developmental lag, a lack of experience or a social/behavioral problem. Careful observation identifies where each child succeeds and where attention is needed.

Working with Parents

Basic educational activities in the home such as cutting, pasting, matching, talking, listening and getting along with other children may provide needed practice for the child. Through parent/teacher communication, parents may become aware of their importance as the first educators of their child. If these basic activities have not been mediated for the child in the home, there is a good chance the child may appear "behind" other children in school. The kindergarten curriculum may be able to overcome this lack of experience in the home, depending on the severity of the deficit. In any case, working with parents to assist them in contributing to the maximum development of their child can not be over estimated.

Role of the Teacher

Because the kindergarten teacher is usually the first professional educator the child meets, the teacher's role is crucial in providing (1) appropriate school experiences in which the child can experience success and (2) adequate diagnosis of need. The teacher must always beware of labeling children. As described earlier in the book, effective teaching:

- gives children ample opportunity to succeed in a range of activity and materials;
- continually assesses where children progress along the continuum of growth domains;
- encourages success by matching children's levels of development with the levels of activity provided;
- assumes children enrolled in any kindergarten program will represent a range of developmental differences.

Teachers model acceptance or rejection of a child for the rest of the children in the classroom. When the teacher responds to a child as being "clumsy," "disruptive," "unable to succeed" or "demanding" of the teacher's time," this misunderstanding will most likely be shared by children in the room. on the other hand, when the teacher treats the child as challenging and capable of succeeding at some level, others will be convinced of this as well.

Making Appropriate Referrals

When diagnostic teaching based on child observations and parental communication do not increase a child's performance, and then appropriate professional referral becomes essential to determine in what setting and how the child may be best taught. Working with school system personnel to confirm the exceptional need of a child is most important. In all states, children with special needs beyond the average population of children include those who are mentally retarded, hard of hearing and deaf, speech impaired, visually handicapped, seriously emotionally disturbed, multi-handicapped, hospital homebound, deaf-blind, have specific learning disabilities and are gifted.

Following the diagnosis of exceptional need by school system personnel, recommendations for work with that child in the classroom may include:

- allowing additional time for the child to complete activities;
- providing special equipment to complete activities (e.g. special magnifying devices for sight or hearing);
- providing a special setting or increased interaction between the adult and child.

Communicating Special Needs to Other Children

Teachers should openly talk about exceptional needs with the other children in the classroom. All children need to feel they are a vital part of the class and can participate to the best of their ability in classroom activities.

Like adults, some children tend to overprotect children with special needs. Children need to understand the circumstances surrounding the special condition of a child and learn how to work constructively with that child. Understanding that these children should be independent in their interactions in the classroom is extremely important. Special accommodations may be needed for these children.

Understanding how each individual in the classroom can most helpfully function under these conditions will set the stage for a maximum learning environment for all children.

- Many handicapping conditions are reversible.
- The earlier the recognition of a special need and provision for that

need, the better the chance of making school success possible for the child.
- Diagnostic teaching is necessary to identify and significantly affect whatever the special need of a child may be.
- Avoid labeling.
- Every child, no matter what the level of development or condition, needs to experience support and success in the classroom.

Program Evaluation Checklist

Program Evaluation: Learning Environment

	Yes	No	Notes
Planning			

Long range planning is used to

A. Organize curriculum units, bases on Selection of objectives for individual child growth.	( )	( )	
B. Organize materials in advance.	( )	( )	

Long rang planning is based on objectives Sequenced along a continuum of child Growth and development in the areas of:

A. Physical development	( )	( )	
B. Intellectual development	( )	( )	
C. Affective development	( )	( )	

The Uses of Objectives

A. State objectives in a sequence of simple forms.	( )	( )	
B. Is used for planning children's daily activities.	( )	( )	

Daily planning sessions

A. Occur at a regular time each day	( )	( )	

	Yes	No	Notes

B.   Involve teachers and aides   ( )   ( )

The planning session includes

A.   Selecting objectives based on children's   ( )   ( )
observed activity.

B.   Developing learning centers and activities   ( )   ( )
Based on objectives matched to the need
of an individual child or group of children.

C.   Selecting practical means of observing and   ( )   ( )
recording child growth in active learning
and settings.

D.   Consideration of all three areas of child   ( )   ( )
Growth (physical, intellectual, affective).

E.   Consideration of children's ideas about   ( )   ( )
what should be learned or experienced.

F.   Identification of how each member of   ( )   ( )
the instructional team will function in
the classroom.

<u>Implementation</u>

The physical space in the classroom

A.   Is arranged into well-defined learning   ( )   ( )
centers.

B.   Motivates children to participate in a   ( )   ( )
wide range of activities.

C.   Encourages and supports an active   ( )   ( )
learning environment.

D.   Reflects the cultural background of the   ( )   ( )
Children (bulletin boards, books,
equipment).

	Yes	No	Notes

Adults in the classroom

A. Interact positively with individual children ( ) ( )

B. Observe individual children. ( ) ( )

C. Give suggestions and support to a child who needs help. ( ) ( )

D. Give feedback to children about their work. ( ) ( )

E. Record activity and growth of children. ( ) ( )

F. Accept and use children's out of school interests (television, toys, games, etc.) as learning activities. ( ) ( )

Teachers involve children in the planning and assessment process by encouraging children to:

A. Talk about what they have done in the classroom during whole group discussion, small group discussion, individual conference. ( ) ( )

B. Suggest activity themes and materials for use in the classroom. ( ) ( )

C. Help develop classroom rules. ( ) ( )

Teachers support children's thinking by:

A. Listening to children's ideas. ( ) ( )

B. Verbally acknowledging children's activity. ( ) ( )

C. Accepting the language and ideas of children. ( ) ( )

D. Extending ideas of children. ( ) ( )

E. Asking open-ended questions. ( ) ( )

	Yes	No	Notes

Evaluation

	Yes	No
A variety of recording methods are used to record individual child growth.	( )	( )

Daily evaluation sessions are held with:

	Yes	No
A. Individual children.	( )	( )
B. Small groups of children.	( )	( )
C. The entire class.	( )	( )
During evaluation sessions, teacher, communication focuses on the strengths of the child.	( )	( )
During evaluation sessions, the child is made aware of needed improvements.	( )	( )
A child's success is based on personal level of development as related to the continuum of objectives.	( )	( )

Scheduling

The daily schedule provides

	Yes	No
A. Planning time for children.	( )	( )
B. Planning time for instructional personnel.	( )	( )
C. Time to observe and assess child growth.	( )	( )
D. Time blocks of one hour or more for learning Center activity in which children are responsible for self-initiated and self-regulated activity selection.	( )	( )

	Yes	No	Notes

E.   There is a balance between:

> independent exploratory/discovery activities.   ( )   ( )

> vigorous plan and less active play.   ( )   ( )

> indoor and outdoor activity.   ( )   ( )

The daily schedule identifies

A.   Time blocks.   ( )   ( )

B.   Learning center themes and activities.   ( )   ( )

C.   Materials or equipment needed at each learning center.   ( )   ( )

D.   Daily routines (i.e., snack time, bathroom break; lunch money collection, etc.   ( )   ( )

Learning Centers

The classroom is organized into four or more of the following learning center areas: ( )   ( )

A.   Construction Center   ( )   ( )

B.   Library Area   ( )   ( )

C.   Cooking Center   ( )   ( )

D.   Game Center   ( )   ( )

E.   Block Center   ( )   ( )

F.   Art Center   ( )   ( )

G.   Dramatics Center   ( )   ( )

	Yes	No	Notes
H. Computer Center	( )	( )	
I. Other	( )	( )	
Each center is organized around a theme.	( )	( )	
Learning centers	( )	( )	
A. Introduce new concepts and skills.	( )	( )	
B. Practice concepts and skills.	( )	( )	
C. Assist each child to take responsibility for his or her own learning.	( )	( )	
D. Provide a variety of activity choices to enhance individualized instruction.	( )	( )	
E. Integrate physical, affective and intellectual development.	( )	( )	
F. Provide independent exploratory/discovery learning experience.	( )	( )	
Activity options at each center account for a Range of child levels.	( )	( )	
In managing learning centers:			
A. Whole group or small group planning sessions are used to introduce learning centers to children.	( )	( )	
B. Expectations for children's behavior at the centers are clearly communicated to children.	( )	( )	
C. Children use a management system that Limits the number of participants in each center (i.e. packet chart, choice board, etc.)	( )	( )	

	Yes	No	Notes
D. There are enough centers in the room for all children to be involved, limiting each to five or less participants at any one time.	( )	( )	

Materials located at each center:

	Yes	No	Notes
A. Relate to the center theme.	( )	( )	
B. Extend individual growth of children.	( )	( )	
C. Support a range of child levels.	( )	( )	
D. Are primarily manipulative.	( )	( )	
E. Can be used successfully by the children.	( )	( )	

Evaluation of child growth at learning centers is obtained.

	Yes	No	Notes
A. As adult interests with child during activity.	( )	( )	
B. As an adult observes child.	( )	( )	
C. By reviewing work child has completed at the center.	( )	( )	
D. By holding conferences with child.	( )	( )	

<u>**The Teaching Team**</u>

The teaching team consists of a teacher certified in early childhood education and a teaching assistant.

During the daily planning and evaluation Sessions, the teacher and teacher assistant

	Yes	No	Notes
A. Exchange specific behavioral observations of children.	( )	( )	

	Yes	No	Notes

B.   Record relevant information about children.   ( )   ( )

C.   Select and plan learning activities for the next day.   ( )   ( )

D.   Identify adult roles and responsibilities in the classroom for the next day.   ( )   ( )

The teacher and teacher assistant:

A.   Know and accept a common philosophy concerning the education of young children.   ( )   ( )

B.   Share routines and clerical chores.   ( )   ( )

C.   Feel comfortable about openly expressing ideas, suggestions and concerns to each other.   ( )   ( )

The instructional teaching team systematically takes responsibility for communicating with The following about program operation:

A.   Parents   ( )   ( )

B.   Principal   ( )   ( )

C.   Supervisors   ( )   ( )

D.   Other kindergarten teachers   ( )   ( )

E.   Primary grade teachers   ( )   ( )

F.   Librarian   ( )   ( )

G.   Psychological services staff   ( )   ( )

H.   Social workers   ( )   ( )

I.   Secretaries   ( )   ( )

		Yes	No	Notes
J.	Custodial staff	( )	( )	
K.	Curriculum Specialist I. Guidance Counselors	( )	( )	

The teaching team systematically takes responsibility for communicating with the following about individual children:

		Yes	No	Notes
A.	Parents	( )	( )	
B.	Principal	( )	( )	
C.	Supervisors	( )	( )	
D.	Other kindergarten teachers	( )	( )	
E.	Primary grade teachers	( )	( )	
F.	Psychological services staff	( )	( )	

Goals for Teaching Kindergarten

There are many goals for teaching kindergarten. In the kindergarten class, the teacher is a vital element. No other person outside the home has quite as much opportunity for influencing the child's development. The teacher is largely responsible for the child's successful transition from home to school; the one who aptly guides the development of character, helping children to temper freedom with responsibility, cultivating the growth of personality, promoting the art of social living and stimulating the use of mental capacities.

A kindergarten program in which learning is fruitful as well as fun is based on clear goals.

The first goal is physical. Goal areas have been identified for each of the major physical development goals. For each goal area, a continuum of objectives and suggested activities has been developed to meet the physical development needs of children with a range of ability.

The following objectives and activities are suggested for implementing with kindergarten children:

- Goal – Gross Motor Development
- Goal Area – Static Balance
- Continuum of Objectives

1. The child will explore a variety of nonlocomotor movements in which the body remains in one position.
2. The child will use different part of the body as a base of support.
3. The child will use a combination of nonlocomotor movements with stability.

- Goal Area – Dynamic Balance
- Continuum of Objectives

1. The child will maintain balance while exploring a variety of locomotor movements.
2. The child will make smooth transitions when changing directions, landing, stopping and starting locomotor movements.

3. The child will use a combination of locomotor movements with stability.

- Goal Area – Gross Motor Coordination
- Continuum of Objectives

4. The child will explore various ways to move from one place to another in a coordinated way.
5. The child will be able to move in various speeds, direction, levels and rhythms.
6. The child will be able to combine movements with a variety of equipment.
7. The child will be able to coordinate movements with those of another child.

- Goal Area – Agility and Endurance/Strength
- Continuum of Objectives

8. The child will explore different amounts of force that can be used with locomotor movements.
9. The child will participate in sustained vigorous activity.

- Goal Area – Arm and Hand Precision
- Continuum of Objectives

10. The child will explore various ways to move the arms and hands.
11. The child will explore various ways to move the arms and hands in combination with different types of equipment.

- Goal Area – Hand and Finger Dexterity
- Continuum of Objectives

12. The child will explore a variety of nonlocomotor movements in which the body remains in one stable position
13. The child will explore various ways the hands and fingers can manipulate different types of objectives.

Suggested Activities

1. The child will explore a variety of nonlocomotor movements in which the body remains in one stable position.

- Give children directions for bending, stretching, turning or twisting individual body parts (e.g., "Put your ear close to your shoulder." "How high can you reach?" "Turn as many ways as you can on one foot.") This might be played as a "Simon Says" game.
- Show children pictures of objects or animals (e.g., tree, elephant, frog, windmill). Have them imitate the position and movement of the picture.

2. The child will be able to use different parts of the body as a base of support.

- Give verbal challenges for body positioning (e.g., "Make the whole front of your body touch the floor. Touch the floor with just two body parts." Balance without your feet touching the floor.")
- Goal – Communication Arts
- Goal Area – Listening
- Continuum of Objectives

3. As an active listener, the child will participate willingly in oral activities.

4. The child will recognize and discriminate among common sounds.

5. The child will demonstrate understanding of a basic vocabulary related to the environment.

6. The child will listen and respond appropriately to language presented orally to furnish information.

7. The child will listen and respond appropriately to language presented orally to furnish information.

8. The child will listen and respond appropriately to language presented orally for the purpose of making judgement.

- Goal Area – Speaking
- Continuum of Objectives

9. The child will use oral language frequently and with enjoyment.

10. The child will develop a speaking voice, which is easy to understand and appropriate to specific situations.

11. The child will build a functional vocabulary related to experience.

12. The child will use elaborated language to describe objects, events, feelings and their relationships.

13. The child will use elaborated language to communicate with others.

   • Goal Area – Reading
   • Continuum of Objectives

1. The child will demonstrate interest in being read to as a way to enrich personal experience.

2. The child will discriminate auditory similarities and differences in commonly used words.

3. The child will discriminate visual similarities and differences in commonly used words.

4. The child will analyze and interpret pictures of objects, people and events using elaborated language.

5. The child will demonstrate understanding of terms used in reading instruction (e.g., top of page, left to right progression, same-different, beginning-ending of words).

6. The child will recognize alphabet letters, words and phrases that appear frequently in the environment.

   • Goal Area – Writing
   • Continuum of Objectives

7. The child will demonstrate interest in a variety of written materials.

8. The child will demonstrate fine motor coordination in a variety of situations.

9. The child will dictate meaningful information to an adult.

10. The child will demonstrate understanding of the left to right pattern of writing.

11. The child will print name and other meaningful words using upper and lower case letters.

- • Goal Area – Visual Arts
- • Continuum of Objectives

1. The child will use art media with case and enjoyment.

2. The child will produce work that is personally satisfying.

3. The child will learn technical aspects of working with various materials and tools.

4. The child will properly care for materials and tools.

5. The child will produce work, which communicates thoughts and feelings.

6. The child will become sensitive to and enjoy art.

7. The child will increase the ability to produce things more realistically.

- • Goal Area – Music and Listening
- • Continuum of Objectives

8. The child will become familiar with and explore different types of music (exploration).

9. The child will identify different notes played on instruments (integration).

- • Goal Area – Music and Singing
- • Continuum of Objectives

10. The child will learn to sing on pitch within a limited range.

11. The child will respond to a request in song.

12. The child will sing spontaneously during activities.

13. The child will create songs.

   • Goal Area – Music and Playing Instruments
   • Continuum of Objectives

14. The child will explore a variety of instruments.

15. The child will be able to play a simple beat or tune.

16. The child will compose music on an instrument.

   • Goal Area – Music and Movement
   • Continuum of Objectives

17. The child will develop the ability to interpret music through body movements, impersonations and dramatizations.

18. the child will develop a vocabulary of fundamental movement (e.g., walking, running, skipping).

   • Goal Area – Dramatic Play
   • Continuum of Objectives

1. The child will express experiences and ideas through action and words.

2. The child will use a variety of props and costumes appropriately.

3. The child will plan a sequence of actions to assume a role in agreement with others.

   • Goal Area – Creative Dramatics
   • Continuum of Objectives

4. The child will pantomime familiar actions and characters with little to no dialogue.

5. The child will act out familiar actions and characters with dialogue.

6. The child will dramatize poems and nursery rhymes.

7. The child will assume the role of a character in a familiar story.

8. The child will sequence actions in a familiar story.

9. The child will work with others in a dramatizing a story.

- Goal Area – Number and Numeration
- Continuum of Objectives

1. Classification. The child will be able to group objectives according to similarities.

2. Serration. The child will be able to arrange objects or events in some kind of order based on differences among them.

3. Matching one-to-one. The child will be able to identify "how many" by matching objects from one set with objects of another set.

4. Recognition and naming of number groups. The child will be able to recognize a set of one, a set of two, a set of three, etc.

5. Counting. The child will be able to recognize and name sets in order as they increase by one.

6. Combining and separating sets. The child will be able to combine and separate sets with different properties.

7. Reading numerals. The child will be able to interpret symbols that represent number properties.

8. Writing numerals. The child will be able to write symbols that represent number properties.

- Goal Area – Measurement
- Continuum of Objectives

9. Comparing and ordering. The child will be able to make statements about the relationship of at least two objects.

10. Using non-standard units to measure. The child will be able to use a go-between device (e.g., hand, foot, paperclip, and string) to measure things.

11. Using standard units to measure. The child will be able to use standard measurement tools such as cups, measuring sticks, scales, clocks, and thermometers.

   - Goal Area – Geometry
   - Continuum of Objectives

12. Awareness of body in space. The child will be able to move in space without fear, receive and give directions for getting from one point in space to another and judge distance to a specific place.

13. Geometric figures and solids. The child will be able to identify, sort and construct geometric figures and solids.

   - Goal Area – Money
   - Continuum of Objectives

1. Recognition. The child will be able to recognize coins and bills as representing a value for exchange.

2. Naming. The child will be able to name common coins and bills.

3. Value. The child will be able to understand the value of each piece of money and associate specific number values with specific pieces of money.

   - Goal Science
   - Goal Area – Observation
   - Continuum of Objectives

4. The child will observe a variety of concrete objects.

5. The child will talk about the observation.

6. The child will use observations to solve problems and draw conclusions.

7. The child will combine parts of previous observations to solve new problems.

8. The child will evaluate the observations while making knowledgeable and thoughtful judgements about the value and purpose of the observations.

   - Goal Area – Classification
   - Continuum of Objectives

9. The child will talk about likeness and differences in objects and events.

10. The child will group like objects and events.

11. The child will combine previous experiences to more precisely group and classify objects or events.

12. The child will evaluate classifications and make knowledgeable and thoughtful judgements about them.

    - Goal Area – Predicting
    - Continuum of Objectives

13. The child will state a prediction.

14. The child will state a prediction based upon specific previous experience and discussion.

15. The child will state a prediction based upon a number of previous experiences.

16. The child will evaluate a prediction based upon previous knowledge and experience.

    - Goal Area – Reporting
    - Continuum of Objectives

1. The child will be able to recall experience.

2. The child will be able to combine a number of experiences and make conclusions about these experiences.

3. The child will be able to combine a number of experiences and make conclusions about these experiences.

4. The child will be able to evaluate the reporting of an experience.

   - Goal Area – Social Studies
   - Continuum of Objectives

5. The child will understand that people as individuals and groups have rights, which must be respected.

6. The child will assume responsibility for personal behavior and demonstrate behavior that contributes to the welfare of the group.

7. The child will develop the concept of family as a community.

8. The child will understand how individuals live together in groups.

9. The child will develop the idea that a community is a group with small contributing groups. The child will name some contributing groups in the community.

   - Goal Area – Cultural Diversity and Heritage
   - Continuum of Objectives

10. The child will describe special events and customs in his/her own family.

11. The child will describe special events and customs in other families.

12. The child will accept the fact that although people may live, dress, speak, and eat differently, they all have similar needs.

   - Goal Area – Physical Environment
   - Continuum of Objectives

1. The child will be able to label and describe physical features in the community (e.g., hill, mountain, field, meadow, valley, beach, river).

2. The child will be able to talk about how people misuse certain land areas in the community and how to prevent these misuses of the environment.

Resources

Allen, R. B. Language experiences in Communication. Boston: Houghton Mifflin Company, 1976.

Allen, R. V. and Allen, C. Language Experience Activities. Boston: Houghton Mifflin Company, 1976.

Burns, P. C., Broman, B. L. and Lowe, A. L. The Language Arts in Childhood Education (2nd Ed.). Chicago: Rand McNally and Company, 1971.

Boyd, G. A. and Jones, D. M. Teaching Communication Skills in the Elementary School. New York: D. Van Nostrand Company, 1977.

Corcoran, G. B. Language Experience for Nursery and Kindergarten Years. Itasca, Illinois: F. E. Peacock Publishers, Inc., 1976.

Forgan, H. W. The Reading Corner: Ideas, Games and Activities for Individualizing Reading. Santa Monica, California: Goodyear Publishing Company, 1978.

Peterson, C. A. Informal Education: Reading and Language Arts. New York: Center For Applied Research in Education, 1975.

Working With Parents

During the 12 months following kindergarten entrance, the child spends about 500 hours in the whole day kindergarten program. Nine times s many waking hours are spent under the supervision of the parents, friend, babysitter, older siblings, relatives, day care workers, computers or television. When collaboration exists between teacher and parent, the impact of kindergarten is likely to be significant; when there is ignorance about the school's objectives and activities, or about the home's values and activities, this brief experience may have minimal significance. Clear communication and mutual understanding between teacher and parent will enhance the program's effect on the child.

Importance of Parent Involvement a the Kindergarten Level

Kindergarten may be the child's first contact with an educational program, certainly with "real" school. Consequently, this is a time of some anxiety for the parent, the child and even the teacher. No matter how impoverished, overwhelmed, insecure, most parents want their children to do well in school. It may appear that the parents who want to be involved are those who cause the greatest problems for their children.

The teacher's primary responsibility is to teach children, not parents. However, devoting some energy to helping parents develop their skill and confidence, as their child's home teacher is likely to have both immediate and long-term benefits for that child and for younger siblings.

Setting the Stage for Parent Involvement

Parent involvement begins with the school's first contact with the parent. Parent participation can be encouraged or discouraged during these early contacts. Impress on parents the importance their behavior plays in what their child learns. Many parents are unaware that in their informal interactions with the child they are actually teaching. Make sure parents feel they still play a very important role in their child's learning, even though the child is enrolled in a classroom program.

Administration of the assessment and screening tests is another of these important early contacts. Since screening instruments will be closely related to program objectives, it may be helpful for parents to observe the testing session. Parents can be briefed about how they are to behave during testing. In a subsequent feedback session, discuss how to teach for underlying processes rather than the test item. In planning a successful parent involvement program, remember some basic principles:

- For any group of parents, a variety of activities should be available. Different parents have varied needs and interests. A teacher working cooperatively with colleagues in the school can increase the variety of activities available.

- An assessment of parents' needs and interests must be conducted if activities are to reflect parent preferences. Schools, alone, cannot decide what parents need.

- Differing degrees of support may be required to enlist the participation of individual parents. For example, single parents with very young children and without an automobile may require baby-sitting and transportation services. Without such logistical support, their participation might be impossible.

- The preferences and circumstances of the parents should determine location of parent involvement activities. Homes, community centers and churches, as well as the school could be used.

- An ongoing parent involvement program will have to accommodate shifts in parent interest, need and competency. Parents, like children, develop and change. Thus, programs will have to adapt to these changes.

- Reinforcement for parent participation will need to be an integral part of the program. Certificates of appreciation, luncheons, dinners, trading stamps, door prizes donated by local merchants and smocks for regular volunteers are ways of recognizing regular participation. The school PTA or PTO could finance these.

- Each teacher must think realistically about the types of parental involvement activities, which can be implemented in the classroom. Parent conferences, parent meetings and open houses are basic and essential for any classroom. One teacher working alone can probably implement only one additional activity, such as training classroom volunteers, helping parents learn to use home-teaching activities of helping organize discussion groups. However, if two or three teachers agree to collaborate, additional options could be offered.

- The purpose of each of the parent involvement activities must be sharply focused and clearly communicated to the parents. Coming to hear a speaker talk about how to get your child ready for first grade may be less clearly focused than what a parent can do to help children learn to read.

Conducting the Needs Assessment

A brief, one-page questionnaire can outline basic home-school communication activities (conferences, meetings) that parents can expect and it can determine the concerns, preferences, interests and needs of this parent group. It would be well to use such a questionnaire at the beginning of the year and at mid-year to assess changes in parent preferences and interests.

Parent Questionnaire
(Need Assessment)

As your child's kindergarten teacher, I plan to work closely with you to insure that your child gains the most from kindergarten. When the parent and teacher work together, the child seems to feel that important adults care and consequently becomes more interested in learning and in school. I want you to know how your child is doing in school and how you can help him/her continue to learn at home. I also want to know about what you see your child doing and learning at home. If we can share this information you child will benefit. Some activities have been designed so we can exchange this information.

We will have three, ½ hour parent conferences during the year, October, January and April. If at all possible, these will be scheduled at school. Monthly classroom meeting will be held on the third Wednesday of each month except December and May. At most of these, we will be talking in general about what the class is learning and how you can reinforce this learning at home. Topics that interest you may be scheduled for discussion at these meetings.

We have found that much more can be accomplished during the year if parents volunteer to help on some tasks. Please check any of the following activities in which you can help.

_____ 1. Volunteering in classroom for one session each week as a regular volunteer.

_____ 2. Volunteering occasionally to share one activity with the children.

_____ 3. Accompanying the class on filed trips.

_____ 4. Preparing learning materials for the classroom.

_____ 5. Serving as a bus aide.

_____ 6. participating in a short series (four meetings) of discussion groups of parents, scheduled at the convenience of the group. (Topics would be decided by the group but could focus on child-rearing problems, discipline, communicating with your child or working with your spouse to establish joint child-rearing strategies.)

_____ 7. Learning how to use specific learning activities with your child at home.

_____ 8. Serving on a classroom parent committee (two parents needed).

<u>What kinds of special skills do you have</u>? This is a good way for us to share the child's culture and family with others in the class.

_____ 1. Sewing	_____ 8. Canning/preserving
_____ 2. Cooking	_____ 9. Farming/gardening
_____ 3. Woodworking & construction	_____ 10. Weaving, quilting, crocheting
_____ 4. Plumbing	_____ 11. Basket weaving
_____ 5. Auto mechanics	_____ 12. Jewelry making
_____ 6. Playing a musical instrument	_____ 13. Curing and smoking meats
_____ 7. Painting/sculpture	_____ 14. Other crafts (please describe)
	_____ 15. Computer

<u>Please indicate your cultural heritage</u>.

_____ 1. African

_____ 2. Cuban

_____ 3. Mexican

_____ 4. French

_____ 5. Scotch-Irish

_____ 6. German

_____ 7. Southern Mountain

_____ 8. Vietnamese

_____ 9. Chinese

_____ 10. Native American (please

            indicate tribe)

_____ 11. Japanese

_____ 12. Other (please indicate)

_____ 13. No specific ethnic/cultural

            group

Strategies for Increasing Home-School Communication

Open channels of communication are essential to sound teacher/parent relations. Parents expect a warning before a major job is encountered. They also want to know about the successes. Certainly, some parents are more difficult to reach than others are. A variety of strategies will need to be considered.

- School conference
- Home visit
- Telephone call
- Contact by the pupil personnel service workers
- An evening or weekend conference

One fundamental principle should guide our behavior. It is the kindergarten teacher's responsibility to exchange information with parents about children's progress.

Parent Conferences

The individual parent-teacher conference is probably the most effective way that teachers and parents have found to share information. To conserve the teacher's time, these are usually conducted at school, although an occasional home visit may need to be made. For either, good preparation will ensure a successful conference.

Preparation

The teacher will want to collect, analyze and summarize information about the child's functioning with respect to program objectives. Use and study anecdotal records, checklists, norm-referenced and criterion-referenced tests you have available then decide what is the most relevant and important information to share. Problem areas should be presented concisely. Discuss emergent skills and achievements, areas where the parent can most easily provide help to the child and can readily see progress.

The conference should be conducted at a place and time convenient to both teacher and parent. If a home visit is planned, parents should be asked to reserve this time exclusively for the teacher with no distractions from neighbors, relatives or salespersons.

The conference should be scheduled well in advance, with a reminder note or phone call prior to the conference.

Conducting the Conference

1. Establish rapport. Describe a humorous incident in the classroom.

2. Start by telling the good news. The child's progress, what she/he has learned.

3. Present problem areas concisely.

4. Wait at each point for the parent's comment.

5. Listen to how they see the child's strengths and problems. Acknowledge that you hear this.

6. Consider a plan of action and commit yourselves to it.

7. Set a time for follow-up evaluation.

8. Summarize the major points of the conference.

Parent Meetings

Group meetings provide a sound strategy for sharing similar information with many people at once. Such meetings can promote peer support systems or social networks in the parent group. As parents come to know and trust one another, support for the development and maintenance of more appropriate parenting behavior can be established. Programs like Alcoholics Anonymous, Parents Anonymous, and Weight Watchers have exploited this principle to effect and maintain dramatic changes in behavior. Surely schools can use the same principle to help parents become more effective facilitators of their children's development.

Topics for meetings might include the following:

- The program goals and objectives
- Buying safe, durable Christmas toys
- How to avoid your child becoming a fat adult
- Living sanely with your children.

Newsletters

In a one-page monthly newsbrief, a variety of information can be provided and events described.

- Field trips
- Class visits by community people
- Class projects or visits
- Community events
- Home activities other parents have tried successfully
- Summaries of newspaper and magazine articles on health, nutrition or child rearing.

Initially, the teacher may have to function as editor. Later a parent could be asked to assemble it. A short newsletter is more likely to be produced and read. Later it might be expanded, as parents are convinced of its utility.

Training Parents as Home Teachers

Enhancing the quality of interaction between parent and child is a worthy goal. Extensive research about parent-child interaction suggests that parents teach their children informally. Several parent focused early childhood programs use basic individual or group consultation strategies. The individual consultation models generally use the home visit in which a parent educator demonstrates learning activities and materials to the parent. In a group consultation model, small groups of parents meet weekly to discuss how to use training materials with their children.

Time limitations may force the classroom teacher to use a group consultation approach simply because it is more efficient.

Certainly a possible alternative involves full-time teachers working with children during the morning session and then working with the parents in the afternoons, evenings and on weekends. Several other strategies might be used.

A Toy Lending Library

In this strategy, commercial toys, games and books have been selected to help children master specific physical, intellectual and effectual skills. The parent learns alternate uses of these materials in order to most effectively meet the child's particular developmental level. One toy is checked out at a time. Such a program might operate as a part of the school library or in the kindergarten classroom. Puzzles, lotto games, Lego, tinker toys, cuisinaire rods, table blocks and pan balance with weights might be available for borrowing.

A Parent Workroom

Obviously, many commercially available materials could be home made. Several recent books provide parents with guidelines for making and using such materials; some of these are listed in the curriculum resource section.

In this parent workroom, "found" materials such as coffee cans, egg cartons, TV dinner plates, poster paper, construction paper, glue and string could be available. Directions for making home learning games would also be provided. The Librarian and the parent assistant could help parents select an appropriate learning game to make for their child.

Home Learning Episodes

Learning episodes could be distributed weekly to parents who would be encouraged to keep them in a loose-leaf binder. Each episode might follow a similar format. Activities design for physical, intellectual or affective development could be mimeographed on paper of the same color. The classroom teacher would probably prepare these. These might encourage parents to maximize the learning opportunities in their usual household routines of laundry, cooking, doing yard work and washing the car. The following might be one such activity:

- Doing laundry
- Help your children learn while they help you with the laundry
- Have them help sort the clothes
- Talk about why you make the different piles and why a piece belongs to each pile: light vs. dark, delicate vs. heavy-duty
- This is the white pile and this is the dark pile
- You can put your clothes in the piles they belong
- That's right, your T-shirt goes with the whites; your jeans go with the dark clothes
- Good thinking

Afterwards discuss sorting the clothes, loading the washer, starting the machine, adding detergent, drying the clothes, folding them and putting them away. This can help your child learn to order events in time. Make this usual chore fun for both of you. Talk about what you are doing.

Discussion groups provide effective and flexible means for parents to acquire more information about a variety of subjects. "Auerbach's Parents Learn Through Discussion" is a thorough guide for acquiring guest speakers and conducting such discussion groups. To be successful, consider the following:

- Select clearly focused topics
- Select knowledgeable speakers
- Plan time and location of meetings in keeping with parents' preferences
- Plan a short series of meetings rather than a long series
- Provide for babysitting/transportation where needed

A real danger presents itself in any parent involvement program when the same parents are involved in al aspects of the program. This easily causes parent "burn out." The classroom teacher will have to help the participants make realistic commitments without overburdening any one parent.

Tailoring the Program to Different Populations

Too often, parent involvement means mother involvement. The planned activities often do not reflect the interests or skills of fathers. Teachers who make concerted efforts to support paternal involvement and provide a male flavor to some involvement activities are more like to foster father involvement. Some discussion groups might be organized just for men. They might discuss the father" role in the child" development using local psychiatrists, pediatricians, psychologists or educators. Some programs have involved fathers to work nights where furniture has been repaired, painted, classrooms rearranged or playground equipment constructed. Certainly fathers and mothers ought to be involved in similar types of activities; however, same sex meetings might encourage reluctant fathers to join in.

Working Parents

Usually they can participate only in evening or weekend activities. Many of the types of involvement activities that have been discussed could easily occur at those times. It is possible that some working parents may have flexible schedules that would allow them to visit the classrooms once a month. Grandparents may have considerably free time than do the children's parents. Likewise, parents, aunts, uncles, and cousins of the child, especially those retired, could provide assistance in the classroom.

Minority Parents

Cuban-Americans, Native Americans, Vietnamese-Americans, and some Black-Americans may have a culture different from that of the school. Value clarification exercises used in parent meetings and parent discussion groups may help the teacher and the parents to understand these differences and similarities. Many minority parents are concerned that their children develop basic skills, but also want them to develop a healthy self-respect regarding their family culture and that of others. Where the teacher makes a concerted effort to find out about the culture of all of the children in the classroom (their values, customs, recreational activities, celebrations, music, and language) and where she/he systematically incorporates it in the curriculum, minority and majority parents are likely to feel welcome and supportive of the school's program.

The Role of the Administrator in Parent Involvement

The discussion has focused thus far on the classroom teacher's role in working with parents. Certainly this role is central, but the classroom teacher does not possess total responsibility for these activities. If a parent involvement program is to be effective, it cannot be confined to one classroom or to one grade level in the school. If the principal supports the kindergarten teacher's efforts much more can be achieved; a coordinated, continuous, more diversified parent involvement program can be constructed. Other auxiliary personnel in the school may wish to devote part of their time to this effort. Elementary school counselors, social workers, school psychologists, nurses, communication specialists, and librarians have skill and training needed in an effective, diversified and coordinated parent involvement program.

Resources

Books for Parent of Young Children

Bell, T. H. Active Parent Concern: A New Home Guide to Help Your Child Do Better in School. Englewood Cliffs, New Jersey: Prentice Hall, 1976.

Brazelton, T. Berry. Infants and Mothers. New York: Delcorte, 1974.

Brazelton, T. Berry. Toddlers and Parents. New York: Delcorte, 1974.

Coplon, F. (ed.) The Parenting Advisor. Garden City, New York. Anchor Press/Doubleday, 1977.

Dodson, F. How to Parent. Los Angeles: Nash Publishing, 1970.

Gordon, I. Baby Learning Through Baby Play. New York: St. Martin's Press, 1970.

Gordon, I. J. et. al. Child Learning Through Child Play. New York: St. Martin's Press, 1972.

Guides to Parent Involvement

Bennett, L. M. and Henson, O. Keeping in Touch with Parents: Teacher's Best Friends. Austin, Texas: Learning Concepts, 1977.

Honig, A. Parent Involvement in Early Childhood Education. Washington, DC: National Association for the Education of Young Children, 1968.

Lane, M. B. Education for Parenting. Washington, DC: National Association for the Education of Young Children, 1975.

Morrison, S. S. Parent Involvement in the Home, School and Community. Columbus, Ohio: Charles S. Merrill, 1978.

Pickarts, E. and Fargo J. Parent Education: Toward Parental Competence. New York: Appleton-Century-Crofts, 1971.

Taylor, K. W. Parents and Children Learn Together. New York: Teachers College Press, 1968.

Home Teaching Programs

Day, M. and Parker, R. The Preschool in Action. Second Edition. Boston: Allyn and Bacon, 1977.

Giesy, R. A Guide for Home Visitors. Nashville, Tennessee: Demonstration and Research Center for Early Education, 1970.

Gordon, I. J. and Breivogel, W. F. Building Effective Home-School Relationships. Boston: Allen and Bacon, 1976.

Lillie, D. L., Trohanis, P. L. and Goin, K. W. (Eds.) Teaching Parents to Teach: A Guide for Working with the Special Child. New York: Walker and Company, 1976.

Training Parent Volunteers

Brock, H. C. Parent Volunteer Programs in Early Childhood Education. Hamden, Connecticut: Linnet Books, 1976.

McManama, J. An Effective Program for Teacher-Aid Training. West Nyack, New York: Parker Publishing Company, 1972.

Miller, B. L. and Wilmshurst, A. L. Parents and Volunteers in the Classroom: A Handbook for Teachers. San Francisco: R and E Research Associates, 1975.

Guides to Parent Discussion Groups

Auerbach, A. B. Parents Learn Through Discussion: Principles and Practices of Parents Group Education. New York: John Wiley, 1968.

Dinkmeyer, D. and Mckay, G. G. Systematic Training for Effective Parenting. Circle Pines, Minnesota: American Guidance Services, 1977.

Assessing the Children's Growth

A model assessment plan for kindergarten in most states is outlined in this chapter. "Model" implies that this chapter is a guide to teachers and other personnel in school systems. The model does not dictate a teacher or school systems evaluate their assessment plans. The chapter contains recommendations if revisions are necessary. The term assessment, as used in this document, involves two components...screening and on-going evaluation of student progress. Each component uses different instruments and recommends different procedures. The purpose and target population for each component is given in Table 1.

Table 1

	Screening	On-going Education
Purpose	To provide quick and reasonably accurate information on developmental and medical history. To identify children who need comprehensive diagnostic evaluation.	To provide accurate on-going information on the degree to which each child is mastering program goals, for the purpose of planning individualized activities.
Population	All children in a school district who are eligible by age criteria for kindergarten	All children in the kindergarten program.
When	Prior to school entry	Continuously in an educational program.

Flowchart of Kindergarten screening Program

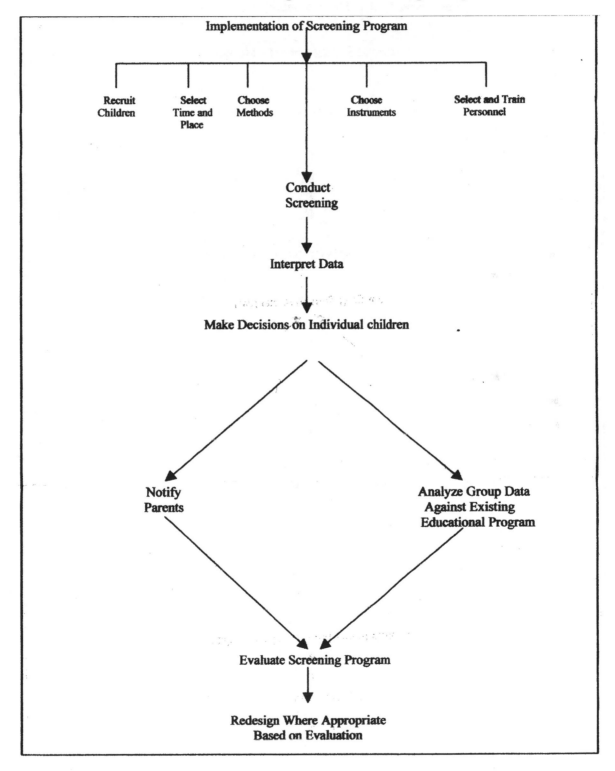

Implementation of Screening Program

Recruit Children | Select Time and Place | Choose Methods | Choose Instruments | Select and Train Personnel

Conduct Screening

Interpret Data

Make Decisions on Individual children

Notify Parents

Analyze Group Data Against Existing Educational Program

Evaluate Screening Program

Redesign Where Appropriate Based on Evaluation

Table II
Flowchart of Kindergarten On-Going Evaluation Component

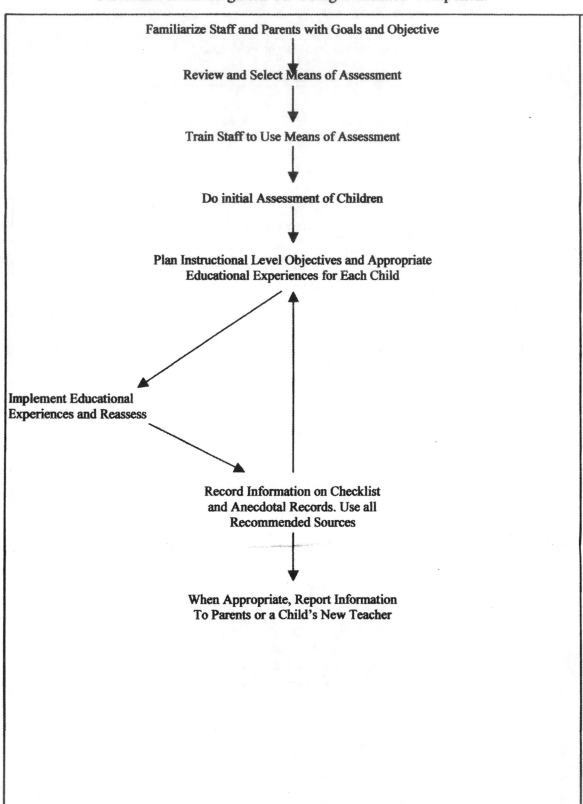

Familiarize Staff and Parents with Goals and Objective

Review and Select Means of Assessment

Train Staff to Use Means of Assessment

Do initial Assessment of Children

Plan Instructional Level Objectives and Appropriate
Educational Experiences for Each Child

Implement Educational
Experiences and Reassess

Record Information on Checklist
and Anecdotal Records. Use all
Recommended Sources

When Appropriate, Report Information
To Parents or a Child's New Teacher

In each section of this chapter the following format is used:

- A flow chart illustrating the component
- Criteria to evaluate current procedures
- Recommended procedures
- Criteria to evaluate currently used instruments
- Recommended instrument.

Developmental Screening for the Kindergarten

The purpose of kindergarten screening in most states is to identify children who need comprehensive diagnostic evaluations. This screening will typically occur in the spring to identify the kindergarten population of the next school year.

Criteria for Evaluating Screening Procedures

- Do personnel in the district understand the purpose of screening as defined in this document?
- Are screening data being misused (e.g. labeling, diagnosis or planning individual educational objectives)?
- Does the person directing screening have the necessary time and experience?
- Are most eligible children screened?
- Are recruitment procedures simple and systematic?
- Do parents have easy access to screening times and locations?
- Are screening locations adequately staffed?
- Are testers adequately trained?
- Are children screened for developmental problems in all areas… intellectual, physical, affective, vision and hearing?
- Are decisions made about the results of screening in an objective and reliable manner?
- Are parents notified of results promptly?
- Does the school district systematically evaluate its screening efforts to improve them.

Recommended Screening Procedures

The following procedures are listed in chronological order:

Choose director.

The director should possess or have access to persons who posses:

- expertise in the areas of measurement, instrument selection, instrument data interpretation, and instrument administration, as these topics relate to the screening of young children.

- familiarity with the community and its resources such as parent or church groups.
- the ability to communicate effectively with parents.
- Familiarity with referral and diagnostic services and procedures.

Evaluate and select instrument(s).

- Currently used instruments should be evaluated and either retained or replaced by recommended instruments.

Recruit children.

- Use media announcements, posters and letters to parents. All recruitment information should be positive in tone. Do not use such phrases as "screening for the handicapped."

Select times and places.

- If possible, have parents make screening appointments. Otherwise, devise some system to avoid long waiting times for parents and children.
- Provide transportation if needed. Use PTA, PTO, or other community service groups.
- Choose locations convenient to all areas of a district.

Select and train personnel.

- Personnel should have experience working with young children.
- All personnel should be adequately trained.
- Each screening location should always have on site a person trained in assessment, such as a speech therapist, psychologist or psychiatrist.

Plan method.

- The purpose and possible outcomes of the screening should be clearly explained to the parents.
- Children should be encouraged but not forced to separate from their parents.

Interpret screening data.

- After a child has been screened, one of three decisions should be made on each child.

The screening results should stand.

> The child should be re-screened. This is done if specified by an instrument's procedure manual, or if there are serious questions about the screening's validity for a particular child and the circumstances are felt to be transitory. The screening results should stand, and the child should be referred for further assessment and diagnosis. If complete diagnostic evaluation is indicated, existing district policies and procedures should be followed.

- When screening is complete, all children screened should be assessed using a common and objective operational definition of greatest developmental need.
- All parents should be notified of the results of the screening.

Follow-up

- After a district has screened children, the group's data should be reviewed. These children will soon be of mandatory school age and screening data can help in projecting future enrollment and educational needs.
- A post-evaluation of screening procedures should make recommendations for change. Parents, screeners and teachers should be among the persons evaluating the screening program.

Administrative Characteristics

The following questions related to test administration should be considered:

1. Can the instrument be administered by a paraprofessional with relatively little training?

2. Can the instrument be administered in a relatively short time?

3. Can the instrument be administered in a non-isolated setting?

4. Are the administration procedures standardized?

5. Does the instrument require a simple response mode such as pointing or short verbal responses?

6. Can the instrument be simply and manually cored in a short amount of time?

Technical Properties

The following questions related to the technical aspects of testing should be considered:

1. Does the instrument yield a score that can be used in ranking children?

2. Can the instrument be scored objectively?

3. Does the instrument have high test-retest reliability?

4. Does the instrument have high validity in its ability to predict the need for further diagnosis?

Recommended Instruments for Screening

Each of the following instruments meets the criteria for screening kindergarten children in most states:

5 <u>Developmental Indicators for the Assessment of Learning (DIAL)</u>

Carol D. Mardell and Dorothy Goldenburg
Childcraft Education Corporation
20 Kilmer Road
Edison, NJ 08817
Kit: $125.00 for all materials for testing 50 children. Cost reduces after initial purchase to $.10 per child for materials.
Purchase includes a training videotape.

<u>General Concepts</u>. The DIAL is designed to identify children with potential learning problems. This pre-kindergarten screening test assesses development in the areas of gross motor, fine motor, concepts, communications and social-emotional development. Scores are established so that the use of DIAL will result in 10 to 15 percent of children screened being referred for further diagnosis.

Age Range [2 ½ to 5 ½ years]

Time Required. The test is not timed. The authors claim it takes 25 to 30 minutes per child to administer all four sub-tests. When using four stations for the sub-tests, six to eight children can be examined per hour. This takes into account three to four children taking different sub-tests at the assigned stations simultaneously.

Conditions of Administration. Although the sub-tests are administered individually, the manual explicitly describes how the screening of many children may be conducted using a station approach. The manual provides detailed information regarding procedures and staffing (team member responsibilities, physical facilities, floor plans, orientation and the use of parents.) Training of each team member two to four hours is essential for a uniform and valid assessment.

Standardization, Reliability and Validity. The DIAL was standardized on 4,356 children. A stratified sample was drawn in the state of Illinois to assure appropriate representation of children on the basis of sex, region, race and socio-economic status. The manual indicates that a balanced population was selected.

A sample of 520 children was used to evaluate test-retest reliability. Although the procedure used by the authors is somewhat ambiguous, and reliability co-efficiency is not reported, the authors state that high reliability was obtained after re-administration of the instrument in one year. Inter-rate reliability is also reported as being high (.81 to 99). A sample of 16 individuals was used in the inter-rate reliability study.

To verify the concurrent validity of the DIAL, a sample of 12 children was selected and tested with the DIAL. Following administration of the test, a diagnostic team of pupil personnel services evaluated the same 12 children. Results of this study yield 85.3 percent agreement between the DIAL scores and diagnostic evaluation date.

Criterion related validity was established by comparing readiness or achievement test scores, DIAL scores and teacher ratings. The sample consisted of 85 kindergarten and 163 first graders. Data were collected from the Iowa Test of Basic Skills, Metropolitan Achievement Test, Metropolitan Readiness Test, and Stanford Achievement Test. Correlation between DIAL categories and achievement scores ranged from 49 to 73.

Comprehensive Identification Profess (CIP) by R. Reid Zehrbach

Scholastic Testing Service, Inc.
480 Meyer Road
Bensonville, IL 60106
Kit: $59.95 including enough material to screen 35 students. Cost reduces after initial purchase.

General Concept. The CIP is designed for locating, screening and evaluating handicapped children. The CIP process, according to the author, results in the identification of more children with mild to moderate problems that would be identified through the traditional agency referral method. Scores are established so that the use of the CIP will result in 10 to 15 percent of children screened being referred for further diagnosis. Percentages may be higher for some states kindergarten population. CIP screens fine motor, gross motor, cognitive-verbal, speech, expressive language, hearing, vision, socio-affective behavior, and a medical history.

Age Range [2 ½ to 5 ½ years of age]

Time Required. No portion of the test is timed. The manual suggests that 30 minutes be allocated for the entire screening assessment. Six to eight children per hour can be examined in stations.

Conditions of Administration. Although CIP may be individually administered, it is designed for giving at a central location using a team approach. Team members can be trained to use the CIP in four to six hours. The author suggests that the individual interviewing the child be experienced in child development. Scoring and administration procedures are standardized. During the time the child is participating in the screening evaluation, the parents are interviewed concerning the child's medical and developmental history. The CIP is currently being translated into Spanish and may also be available in French shortly.

Standardization, Reliability and Validity. The CIP has been developed and evaluated on an Illinois population of over 700 children. The author states that the sample was cross-cultural, comprised of white, black, and Asian children. A description of this ample is not reported. Reliability co-efficiency was also unreported although the author states that inter-rater reliability is quite good.

To evaluate whether of not the CIP results provide accurate judgements for student referral, a sample of children was administered the test. Traditional referral agencies or personnel, social workers, physicians, speech and language therapists, and school psychologist evaluated the children identified as needing a complete work-up. A comparison was made between the characteristics of children referred by the CIP and the traditional mode of identification. There were no significant differences between the mean age of the groups or sex in regards to the two methods of identification. It was determined that I. Q. differences existed between the two groups and children referred by the traditional method seemed to be more severely handicapped than those referred by CIP.

Denver Developmental Screening Test
William K. Frankenburg, Josiah B. Dodds, Alma Fandel
University of Colorado Medical Center

Laradon Hall Publishing Company
East 51st, Avenue and Lincoln
Denver, CO

Kit: $7.00 for complete kit; test forms $2.00 and 100 manuals $4.00

General Concepts. The Denver Developmental Screening Test is designed to aid in the early discovery of children with developmental problems in the areas of personal social, fine motor adaptive, language and gross motor.

Age Range. One month to six years of age.

Time Required. No portion of the Denver Developmental Screening Test is timed. It appears that two to three children can be tested per hour.

Conditions of Administration. This individually administered screen can be used by paraprofessionals with adequate supervision. The manual provides explicit instructions for administering and scoring the instrument.

Because a socio-affective evaluation component built into the instrument requires parental information, parents must respond to items in the first section.

Suggested order for administering the sub-test is Personal, Social, Fine Motor, Adaptive, Language, and Gross Motor.

Standardization, Reliability and Validity. A sample of 1,036 children from Denver ranging in age from two weeks to six years served in the developmental studies.

Percentages of agreement have ranged from 80 to 95 percent for inter-rater reliability. Twenty children were re-tested after a lone week interval in the test-retest reliability study. Agreement of items scored the same way after that interval for the children was 95.8 percent.

In a concurrent validity study, DDST scores were compared to Standard-Binetor Revised Bayley Infant Scales scores. Scores were similar to referrals for instruments used by traditional referral agencies.

Appendices

Appendix A

LIST OF INSTRUMENTS REVIEWED

All of the instruments listed below were reviewed as potential screening or on-going evaluation instruments. The instruments are as follows:

1 American School Reading Readiness Test

2 Animal Crackers

3 Arizona Articulation Proficiency Scale: Revised Assessment of Children's Language Comprehension

4 Boehm Test of Basic Concepts

5 Bowen Language Behavior Inventory

6 Carrow Elicited Language Inventory

7 Child Behavior Rating Scale

8 Circus

9 Comprehensive Evaluation Process (CIP)

10 Comprehensive Skills of Assessment Battery (CSAB)

11 Comprehensive Test of Basic Skills (CTBS)

12 Daily Language Facility Test

13 The Dallas Pre-School Screening Test

14 Denver Developmental Screening Test

15 Pre-School Inventory (Cooperative or Caldwell)

16 Developmental Profile

17 Developmental Test of Visual Motor Integration

18 Developmental Indicators for the Assessment of Learning (DIAL)

19 Fairview Behavior Evaluation Battery for the Mentally Retarded

20 Goldman Fristoe Test of Articulation

21 Goldman Fristoe Woodcock Auditory Skills Test Battery

22 Hannah/Gardneryes Preschool Language Screening Test

23 Inventory of Readiness Skills

24 Learning Accomplishment Profile

25 Lexington Developmental Scale (Short Form)

26 Maturrity Level for School Entrance and Reading Readiness

27 McCarthy Scales of Children's Ability

28 Meeting Street School Screening Test

29 First Grade Screening Test

30 Gressi Basic Cognitive Evaluation

31 Metropolitan Achievement Tests: Revised

32 Minnesota Preschool Scale

33 Motor Free Visual Perception Test

34 Oseretsky Test of Motor Proficiency

35 Peabody Picture Vocabulary Test

36 Preschool Screening Survey

37 Preschool Academic Sentiment Scale

38 Primary Self-concept Inventory

39 Quick Test

40 Santa Clara Inventory of Developmental Task

41 Screening Test for Auditory Comprehension of Language (STACL)

42 School Readiness Survey

43 Screening Test for the Assignment of Remedial Treatment

44 Screening Test for Academic Readiness

45 Slosson Intelligence Test for Children and Adults

46 Southern California Figure Ground Visual Reception Test

47 Speech and Language Screening Test for Preschool Children

48 SRA Primary Mental abilities

49 Thomas Self Concept Values Test

50 Test for Auditory Composition of Language

51 Test of Basic Experiences

52 Utah Test of Language Development

53 Valett Developmental Survey of Basic Learning Abilities

54 Verbal Language Development

55 Vineland Social Maturity Scale

56 Harrison Stroud Reading Readiness Profile

57 Walter Readiness Test for Disadvantaged Preschool Children

58 Stanford Early School Achievement

59 Walker Problem Behavior Identification

Reporting To a Child's Next Teacher or Parent/Guardian

Summary reports should be objective and directly related to program goals. They should help the next teacher or the parent/guardian know where to begin teaching a child. The report should be stated in observable terms and should state the child's most advanced accomplishment in each program area.

Example of a Summary Report

Child's Name _____ Address _____
Birthdate _____ Parent/Guardian _____
Height _____ Telephone No. _____
Weight _____

I. Physical Development

Gross Motor

Static balance…balance on one foot, no supports

Dynamic balance…runs smoothly, walks balance beam with no support

Gross motor coordination…catches volleyball thrown from 6 feet. Throws tennis ball accurately to cohort six feet away.

Fine motor

Arm and hand precision

Hand and finger dexterity

II. Intellectual Development

Science

Observing

Classifying

Predicting

Reporting

Social Studies

[Include other curriculum areas]

States Resources for Teachers of Kindergarten Children Services

The early childhood staffs of each states Department of Education provides the following services to school systems and kindergarten teachers:

1. Staff leadership services to establish and expand states supported and selected preschool programs

2. Technical assistance in selecting appropriate materials and in writing curricula

3. In-service and staff development for administrators and classroom personnel

4. Workshops

5. Assistance to colleges and universities in establishing early child teacher training programs

6. Technical assistance to state agencies and other programs that provide early childhood education

7. Development of states regulations, standards and guidelines for preschool programs

8. Dissemination of information, materials, resources and research to local system

9. Participation on teams and hoc committees for local system self study

10. Development and leadership services for state and local pre-assessment programs

11. Technical assistance and participation in the development of programs for parents and parent involvement

Bibliography

Llen, R. V. and Allen, C. Language Experience Activities. Boston: Houghton Mifflin Company, 1976.

Bertethon, B. and Boardman, E. Musical Growth in the Elementary School. New York: Holt, Rinehart, and Winston, Inc., 1970.

Bloom, B. S., Hastings, J. T., and Madaus, G. F. Handbook on Formative and Summative Evaluation of Student Learning. New York: McGraw Hill Book Company, 1971.

Boyd, G. A. and Jones, D. M. Teaching Communication Skills in the Elementary School. New York: D Van Nostrand Company, 1977.

Bronfenbrenner, U. Two Worlds of Childhood: U.S. and U.S.S.R. New York: Russell Sago Foundation, 1970.

Burns, P. C., Broman, B. L. and Wantling, A. L. The Language Arts in Childhood Education. Chicago: Rand McNally and Company, 1976.

Burns, P. C. and Roe, B. D. Teaching Reading in Today's Elementary Schools. Chicago Rand McNally and Company, 1976.

Butler, A. L. Gotts, E. E., and Quisenberry, N. L. Early Childhood Programs. Columbus, Ohio: Charles E. Merrill Publishing Company, 1975.

Cohen, D. H. and Rudolph, M. Kindergarten and Early Schooling. Englewood Cliffs, New Jersey: Prentice-Hall, Inc. 1977.

Croft, D. J. and Hess, R. D. An Activities Handbook for Teachers of Young Children. Boston: Houghton Mifflin Company, 1975.

Elardo, P. and Cooper, M. Aware: Activities for Social Development. Menlo Park, California: Addison Wesley Publishing Company, 1977.

Foster's and Headley's Education in the Kindergarten (4th ed., rev. by N. E. Headley), New York: American Book Company, 1966.

<u>Round Spaced and Equipment for Children's Centers</u>. New York: Educational Facilities Laboratories, Inc., 1972.

Frost, J. L. <u>Revisiting Early Childhood Education: Readings</u>. New York: Holt, Rinehart and Winston, Inc., 1973.

Hammond, S. L., Dales, R. J. Skipper, D. S., and Winterspoon, R. L. <u>Good Schools for Young Children: A Guide for Working with Three, Four, and Five-Year-Olds</u>. New York: The Macmillan Company, 1963.

Harlan, J. D. <u>Science Experiences for the Early Childhood Years</u>. Columbus, Ohio: Charles E. Merrill Publishing Company, 1976.

Hess, R. D. and Croft, D. J. <u>Teachers of Young Children</u>. New York: Houghton Mifflin Company, 1972.

Ilg, F. and Ames, L. B. <u>Child Behavior</u>. New York: Harper and Row, Publishers, 1975.

Kamili, C. and DeVries, R. <u>Piaget, Children and Number</u>. Washington, DC: National Association for the Education of Young Children, 1970.

Kamili, C. and DeVries, R. <u>Piaget, Children and Number</u>. Washington, D. C.: National_ Association for the Education of Young Children, 1969.

Lillie, D. L. <u>Early Childhood Education: An Individualized Approach to Developmental Instruction</u>. Chicago: Science Research Associates, Inc., 1976.

Lindberg, L. and Swedlow, R. <u>Early Childhood Education: A Guide for Observation and Participation</u>. Boston: Allyn and Bacon, Inc., 1976.

Logan, L. M. <u>Teaching the Young Child: Methods of Preschool and Primary Education</u>. Cambridge, The Riverdale Press, 1960.

Lovell, K. <u>The Growth of Understanding in Mathematics: Kindergarten Through Grade 3</u>. New York: Holt, Rinehart, and Winston, Inc., 1971.

Osmon, F. L. <u>Patterns for Designing Children's Centers</u>. New York: Educational Facilities Laboratories, Inc., 1970.

Robison, H. F. and Spodek, B. <u>New Directions of the Kindergarten</u>. New York: Teachers College Press, Teachers College, Columbia University, 1965.

Rudolph M. and Cohen, D. H. <u>Kindergarten: A Year of Learning</u>. New York: Meredith Publishing Company, 1964.

Schickedanz, J. A., York, M. E., Stewart, I. S. and White, D. <u>Strategies for Teaching Young Children</u>. Englewood Cliffs, N. J.: Prentice-Hall, Inc., 1977.

Smith, J. A. <u>Creative Teaching of the Language Arts in the Elementary School</u>. Boston: Allyn and Bacon, Inc., 1973.

Todd, V. E. and Heffernan, <u>The Years Before School: Guiding Preschool Children</u>. New York: the Macmillan Company, 1970.

Wankelman, W. F., Wigg, P. and Wigg, M. <u>A Handbook of Arts and Crafts for Elementary and Junior High School Teachers</u>. Dubuque, IA: William C. Brown, Publishers, 1968.

Weihart, D. P., Rogers, L., Adcock, C. and McClelland, D., <u>The Cognitively Oriented Curriculum: A Framework for Preschool Teachers</u>. Washington, DC: National Association for the Education of Young Children, 1971.

Assessment

Berman, A. L. D. <u>Resource Materials: The Great Ripoff</u>. Journal of Learning Disabilities, May, 1977, Vol. 10, No. 5, 7-9.

<u>Curriculum Guide for Kindergarten</u>. Tallahassee, FL; University of West Florida Cluster Of the Tri-State Project.

Gearheart, B. R. and Willenberg, E. P. <u>Application of Pupil Assessment Information</u>: For the Special Education Teacher. Denver, CO; Love Publishing Company, 1970.

Gossi, J. A. Pinkstaff, D. Hanley, C., and Stanford, A. R. <u>The Chapel Hill Study of the Impact of Mainstreaming Handicapped Children in Region IV Head Start</u>. Chapel Hill, NC: Lincoln Center, August 1975.

Hoepfner, R., Stern, C., and Nummedal, S. G. CSE-ECRC Preschool/ Kindergarten Test Evaluation. Los Angeles: Center for the Study of Evaluation, 1971.

Johnson, O. G. and Bowman, J. W. Tests and Measurements in Child Development: A Handbook. San Francisco: Jossey-Bass, Inc., 1971.

Mauser, A. J. Assessing the Learning Disabled: Selected Instruments. San Rafael, California: Academic Therapy Publications, 1976.

Miller, E., Lombardi, N., Macleod, J. and Block, H. Developmental Assessment of Young Children: Description of a Multidimensional Battery. (Unpublished Paper).

Procedures for Survey, Screening Evaluation, Placement, and Dismissal of Children Into/Out of Programs for the Handicapped. South Carolina Department of Education, Office of Programs for the Handicapped.

Sanford, A. R., Pinkstaff, D. K., Henley, H. C., and Bondegyns, N. E. The 1976 Chapel Hill Study of Services to the Handicapped in Region IV Head Start. Chapel Hill, NC: The Chapel Hill Outreach Project, Lincoln Center, August 1976.

Screening Evaluation Placement. PEECH Project. (Unpublished Paper, Institute for Child Behavior and Development, University of Illinois, 1977.

Stallings, J. and Wilcox, M. Phase II. Instruments for the National Day Care Cost-Effects Study: Instruments Selection and Filed Testing. Menlo Park, CA: Stanford Research Institute, 1976.

Standards for Educational and Psychological Tests and Manuals. Washington, DC: American Psychological Association, Inc., 1974.

Zehrback, R. R. Determining a Preschool Handicapped Population. (Unpublished Paper, Copyright for the Council for Exceptional Children).

Zeitlin, S. Kindergarten Screening: Early Identification of Potential High-Risk Learners. Springfield, IL: Charles C. Thomas, Publisher, 1976.